# SUNSHINE

## FOREVER & ALWAYS

Nina Nani



BlueRose ONE.com
Stories Matter
NewDelhi • London

**BLUEROSE PUBLISHERS**
India | U.K.



BlueRose ONE.com
Stories Matter
NewDelhi • London

For permissions requests or inquiries regarding this publication, please contact:

BLUEROSE PUBLISHERS
www.BlueRoseONE.com
info@bluerosepublishers.com
+91 8882 898 898
+4407342408967

ISBN: 978-93-5989-001-2

Cover design: Rishav Rai
Typesetting: Rohit

First Edition: March 2024

*In fond memory of a perfect elder brother and a dedication to his life well-lived.*
*We miss you. A little too much, a little too often, and a little more everyday.*

*In life we loved you dearly, in death we do the same*
*Our family chain is broken and nothing seems the same*
*But as God calls us one by one, the chain will link again.*

# Thank you

**My three** cutie patooties: for being my inspiration and my motivation.

**Enayah** -ah! What can I say? You have as many facets to your personality as there are meanings to your name.

In Urdu you are the light of heaven; in Arabic, you represent care and concern; in Farsi your name means blessing.

Thank you, baby, for lending your voice to the **Sunshine Survives** story.

I hope when you read the *fox laid eggs* story, you will recall your narration to me. I had laughed and you were most indignant and had said," It is MY story, Nani. And, in my story - the fox does lay eggs!" I could find nothing better to make King Dareall laugh in **Zurika The Gypsy Princess**.

Thank you, my bestie **Alexander** for helping out in the **Sunshine Survives** opinion section. I am sure the children who read the book will enjoy your views. *Te amo y te extraño*

(I love you and miss you) and promise my next book will have some flavour of Mexico.

Thank you to our little Rockstar **Ryan**, whose dimpled smile melts our hearts. Your observations on **Sunshine Survives** will be most appreciated.

THANK YOU

**My son** – while raising you I was cultivating a garden of potential pride and joy. You have travelled far, towards unbelievable future possibilities. No matter the distance, you carry a piece of my heart with you.

**My daughter** - in your strength, I find inspiration; in your kindness, hope; and in your presence, pure comfort. I now know for sure that you could, perhaps, take a mother out of her daughter but you can never ever take a daughter out of her mother.

**Mamta** – for helping me organise my thoughts, leave fear behind and get started with the editing and publishing process.

**Suman** – IT ALL BEGAN WITH YOU. A long-forgotten passion for writing was reignited. This book bears testimony to your contribution.

**Pimal and Manju** - for helping me source the requisite tools.

**Dr. Edavally Vijayendra Reddy** - for providing me a wonderful, serene workplace where the sunshine is delicious, rain is refreshing, wind bracing and the snow-sighting exhilarating. Here, there is no such thing as bad weather, only different kinds of good weather.

**Adine Roode** - for so graciously allowing Sunshine's story to reach many children.

And of course, THANK YOU **BLUE ROSE ONE** Publishers

**Sameer, Deepika, Devansh Malviya, Rishav, Rohit** - It has been an incredible association. You held my hand and took me through the entire process - seamlessly, efficiently, willingly, kindly and with so much warmth.

# Contents

# Zurika The Gypsy Princess

Once upon a time, in the faraway **Kingdom of Kola,** in a beautiful palace, lived **King Dareall**, with his wife **Queen Iza** and son **Prince Nicholas**.

The prince was six years old and very lonely. He yearned for a sibling. Someone he could play and have fun with.

Around that time, King Dareall lost his best and most loyal courtier, **Chancellor Castro** in a tragic accident. Unfortunately, Chancellor Castro's wife too was killed. The only survivor was **Zurika**, their daughter, who was only one year old. The King and Queen were grief-stricken that beautiful baby Zurika was left orphaned. They decided to bring her up as their foster daughter. Prince Nicholas was thrilled. He loved playing with baby Zurika and enjoyed her cooing and baby behaviour.

Almost four years went by, happily. The King was a merry, kind and generous man and his courtiers and subjects were also a lively, happy lot.

The Kingdom of Kola was becoming increasingly unsafe and the people were feeling more and more unhappy. The problem was with the GYPSIES, a wandering people without a country. They had come in hundreds and taken Kola by storm. No one felt either safe or happy any more. The once-loved gypsy folk had slowly become a nuisance, a threat to the safety and security of the people.

The peaceful and fascinating gypsies, who had earlier been either craftsmen selling unique jewellery, beautiful scarves and lovely painted spoons; or storytellers, who would describe their wondrous travel tales to and from distant lands; or excellent musicians and graceful dancers who could get everyone singing and dancing to songs and melodies never heard before– had now turned into rogues.

Since they rarely remained in one place for more than a month, the people of Kola would, in the earlier days, eagerly await the arrival of a new band of gypsies. They would be excited to see what wares they would have to sell and what new stories they would have to tell. They always looked forward to the excitement the wandering gypsies would bring into their lives.

The gypsies would settle on the outskirts of the Kingdom with their caravans neatly parked. The gypsy camp was a fascinating place that the women and children of Kola would often visit. Gypsies were a merry and lively lot and the place was always full of music, dancing and fascinating activity.

Besides singing and dancing there would be acrobatics and interesting food on sale. The atmosphere was always fun-filled. The gypsies would earn money and live without struggle. The people of Kola were kept entertained. Everyone enjoyed their lives together.

However, this fun and carefree living was now becoming a thing of the past. With each new band of gypsy arrivals, the situation was worsening.

The once colourfully dressed women in ankle-length skirts and shawls and spirited dancing, were replaced with dirty, torn clothes, dishevelled hair, filthy feet and shabby flip-flops.

The gypsies had changed from being wandering vagabonds with values and goodness, into dangerous people. They left behind loss, danger and dirt. Their visits and stay left every area poorer and angrier. They owned nothing, they had nothing and they feared nothing. They no longer wanted to work and earn money. They did not care for any religion, rules or laws. They would rob people, steal from the fields and beat up and kidnap children.

King Dareall and his courtiers had tried everything to stop this nuisance. Sadly – nothing worked.

One day, as King Dareall's court was in session, there was a sudden commotion. Several people ran into the courtroom unannounced, with palace guards close at their heels, trying to stop them. "Your Majesty," said the Head of the People's Council, "terrible things are happening. The marketplace has been attacked by gypsies. They are carrying away all the goods. They are burning down shops and beating up the shop owners and shoppers. They have also attacked the grocery stores and are on the way to loot people's homes. Please help us. We are scared and helpless."

Everyone was stunned. Their happy meeting place and merry marketplace was being looted. Their people had been hurt.

The King's men jumped up, collected their teams and ran towards the attacked spots to fight the violent gypsies. What they saw was horrifying. There was utter chaos and panic everywhere. People were running back home screaming and sobbing. Women wailing, children crying and worried men trying to protect their families from getting hurt.

Pockets were being picked, bags snatched, shops looted, homes plundered, crops stolen and chickens picked up. The gypsies had come prepared with sticks and stones and had brought along carts and carriages to carry back the stolen goods. They were taking everything they could lay their hands on.

The King's men, swinging into action, attacked the robbers. They tried to shoo the gypsies away and also stopped them from running away with the loot. Some soldiers chased on foot. Some fought with swords. Many were on horseback. The really strong ones and brave fighters were using their fists and feet to fob off the attackers.

The Commander was shouting out instructions and soldiers were obeying his orders. After a few hours of fighting, most of the gypsy attackers had been caught. The Prison Attendant arrived and ordered that all the captured gypsies be taken away to prison.

The Chief of the Army ordered that the captured gypsies be crammed into cells and given nothing but bread and water. That too, only after all the stolen goods had been returned. The prisons were soon full.

That night, the town was deserted. Not one person ventured out. They were all locked up in their homes.

The King and his loyal men were huddled in a meeting all night. There was bound to be big trouble. The gypsies would be very angry at being attacked and even angrier at being locked up in jail. They would surely take revenge.

The King was a worried man. Queen Iza was even more so. She was scared that the gypsies would kidnap Prince Nicholas and her sweet little foster child, Zurika. Gypsies are experts at kidnapping rich children, either for ransom or revenge.

In the midst of all this, the King realised that the Royal Doctor and the Royal Priest were not present in court. The courtiers told King Dareall that the doctor had been up all night, tending to the many wounded people and was limping in pain and exhaustion. The priest had been hurt while trying to control the gypsies and calm them down. Stones and sticks had been hurled at him. He was wounded and in poor shape. Shortly after, both the priest and the doctor entered the courtroom.

**Doctor Dano** informed His Majesty King Dareall that all soldiers who were hurt had been treated. Despite many injuries, they had arrived on duty, having locked their families up for safety.

**Priest Palafair** solemny said a prayer while addressing His Majesty the King, "Praise be to the Lord, that none of our people lost their lives yesterday. Let us all pray to Him to continue to save our people." The courtiers stood up to recite a prayer for protection, led by Priest Palafair. By the end of the prayer, many present were seen getting emotional and wiping their tears. It was truly a traumatic and troubled time.

King Dareall now realised that quick action was needed. He requested his men to find a solution as soon as possible. While discussions were still on, there was yet another interruption. Many panic-stricken men barged into the courtroom to inform the King of a frightening thing they had just discovered.

The streets had been deserted as markets had not re-opened. The people were frightened of leaving their homes. The Head of the People's Council and a few strong young men decided to quietly walk around the deserted town to ensure all was well.

The group was aghast at a strange sight outside **Farmer Felaberu Fanibanda's** locked house. The gypsies must have known that the farmer and his family were away attending a family celebration. They had, therefore, tried to break in to steal stuff from Farmer Felaberu Fanibunda's house. Not succeeding in doing so, must have made them furious. Hence, they had left behind a marker on the house, in the form of a pair of scissors inside a pouch wrapped round and round with a woman's elastic hairband. The whole packet was stuffed between the bars of the sealed window.

The men explained to the unknowing courtiers that this was a typical **gypsy curse**, meant to scare people. The gypsies loved to terrorise people and rob them of their possessions. The entire court froze at this revelation.

His Majesty, King Dareall announced, "This is, indeed, a shocking event. But, we will not allow ourselves to be afraid. We will face the situation as bravely as possible and will not rest till we have driven these wretched gypsies out of our Kingdom, never to return."

King Dareall told his army Generals to prepare their soldiers for all emergencies.

He asked his personal **Page Boy Partley** to summon the Town Criers to court.

He instructed his Noblemen to ensure the safety of all women and children.

He asked **Chamberlain Cantor** to ensure that they had enough resources to fight the gypsies.

He urged all the Knights to spend their days and nights on duty.

By the time the Town Criers had arrived, the plans had all been finalised.

The Chief of Staff read out the proclamation to the court and handed out a copy to each of the four Criers, who served as talking newspapers. This was useful, because some people were not educated and could not read.

The first Crier, **Charlie** went to the **town square**. It was from there that he would read out the King's message. Anxious people started hurriedly gathering in the square, eager to know what the King had to tell them.

The second Crier, **CableCar** hurried to **the market place.** It soon started to fill up as people were curious to find out what King Dareall wanted them to know.

The third Crier, **Catapult** took his position at **carnival square.** There, he waited for people from nearby houses to arrive. Soon, women with scared children holding on to their mother's petticoats, came scurrying to hear the latest news from their beloved King.

The fourth Crier, **Caratlane** had to run up and down **the bylanes of Kola** while shouting out the message, for the old and feeble, sick and injured, unable to leave home.

They all rang their bells furiously to get the attention of the people and this is what they said,

*"Hear Ye, Hear Ye, A message that comes from the powers that be*

*10 o'clock all is well. His Majesty the King has much to tell*

*Except for Dr. Dano who can't walk, and Priest Palafair who can't talk*

*All the King's men are hurt but brave, for they know they have you to save*

*The Gypsy King is summoned to court, the King with him will sort it out*

*King Dareall is an angry man, and to the gypsies his wrath will tell*

*Not one of them will he spare, but keep in prison all those who are there*

*Gentle folk, do not fear, the King and His men are always near*

*From gloom and doom you will be spared, to live the life you've always had*

*With the gypsies our connection we will sever*

*Will we allow them in our Kingdom? NEVER EVER!*

*We will fight with all our might, never to them will we show our plight*

*We'll be strong and we'll be fair, and rely on our soldiers who are always there*

*For just a little longer keep your cool, for soon the King will oust these fools.*

***LONG LIVE THE KING, GOD SAVE OUR KING"***

Meanwhile, the Gypsy King who had escaped, was captured and brought to the King's palace. The gypsy camp was raided and the remaining rogues were rounded up. The entire palace was under high security as the gypsies arrived.

There was the **Gypsy King Kamikaze**, his chief assistant **Deputy Damocles**; crafty kidnapper **Grizzly Groa**; heckler **Happy Hella**; raider **Rascal Runar**; killer **Axey Ailes**; tyrant **Terror Thilde** and stealer **Snakey Silvanus**.

There were harsh words exchanged between the two groups. King Dareall was furious. The Gypsy King and his gang were being rough, rude and disrespectful. They continued to threaten the King and his men and refused to apologise and admit to their acts of crime.

Furious at the bad-mannered gang, King Dareall decided to take strong action. He would no longer help get them work to make an honest living. He cancelled their jobs in the local strawberry farms. He also withdrew the privileges that he had given them - like letting them work in the cornfields, paying them to shoo away birds that destroyed crops, collecting hay to help the farmers and helping people repair their houses.

As it is, the gypsies had become so lazy that no one was working anymore. They just wanted to live and eat for free.

Surprised by the King's strong punishment, the gypsies were fretting and fuming as they walked out of court, huffing and puffing. The courtiers were worried the gypsy rogues would do something awful to harm them all. **Gypsies never forget** and always fight back. They are dangerous and ruthless.

King Dareall ordered the prison officials to get more guards so the prisoners could not break out of jail. Since many of the fiercest gypsies were still roaming free, it was a scary situation. He ordered the soldiers to go to the gypsy camp and give them two days to leave the Kingdom. After which time, their camp would be set on fire and those who remained, would be killed. He also asked artists to make placards to keep the gypsies out.

As people were hustling and bustling around to help get things done - suddenly, in the town square appeared this scary, ferocious, demonic, axe-wielding gypsy, **Savage Sandor Sabic**. The people had presumed he had been caught and imprisoned. Clearly, he had escaped. However, the obedient and simple town folk remembered what their King had told them about '**fear**'. They ran at the crazy, devilish Savage Sandor Sabic. They pinned him down, tied him up in ropes and handed him over to the guards who, by then, had arrived at the scene.

The posters warning the gypsies to get out of Kola were put up at every nook and corner of the Kingdom.

The gentler among the gypsy folk had started getting their things together to move out. They were unhappy to leave Kola in search of a new place to pitch their tents and park their caravans. They were sad to leave the lovely Kingdom, the kind King and the gentle people. They had been so happy here and had decided to leave their wandering gypsy life and live on in Kola forever. Alas! The wayward ways of the rogues amongst them, had ruined their plans. They were now being forced out towards the unknown.

Even as the few good, honest, peace-loving gypsies were preparing to leave, a terrible incident was unfolding in the King's palace. Little Zurika and Prince Nicholas were playing, with their bodyguards watching over them. Zurika was now around five years old and Prince Nicholas was eleven. Prince Nicholas decided to get his hobbyhorse. While running to fetch it, he tripped on the stairs. The guards ran to help him. Zurika was left playing hopscotch on the terrace all by herself.

Zurika peered over the parapet and saw a mysterious man beyond the palace grounds and behind the high walls. He was performing amazing magic tricks and whistling to the tune of a song. Zurika found the music magical. She leaned out to look at the man better. He gestured to call her over. Forgetting that she was not allowed to go anywhere without the guards, she quickly ran down the golden steps, to the unmanned gate at the back of the palace grounds. The sly man hauled her over the low gate with one quick swipe, covered her mouth and putting her in a largish bag, took off.

## ZURIKA HAD BEEN KIDNAPPED

Zurika's kidnapping marked the end of happy times in the lives of King Dareall, Queen Isa and Prince Nicholas. The HAPPY Kingdom of Kola ceased to exist. A heavy cloud of loss and sadness had descended. Their very own, adorable

Zurika had been taken away, maybe, never to be seen again! Because the gypsies are notorious thieves, because they are thugs, because they are vagabonds, there was little hope of Zurika ever returning to Kola, alive.

The Kingdom of Kola went on to get rid of the gypsies. The nuisance and noise, the fear and instability were gone. Grief remained.

King Dareall had stopped meeting people

Queen Iza was heartbroken

Prince Nicholas was devastated

The courtiers were very sad

The people were in shock

The kind King who had protected them so zealously, had suffered the loss of his dearest Zurika. Every morning, soldiers would set off in different directions in search of Zurika. Every evening would see one or the other group return empty-handed and disappointed. The King's spies were spread out in all directions, but Zurika remained missing.

Twelve long years passed. The Royals remained sad, the Kingdom and its people in mourning. King Dareall was getting weaker every day. His health was failing. He had not smiled at all since that fateful day. The doctors were worried for him and insisted that all efforts be made to bring the King out of his sadness.

The court would meet every day and the best Jesters were hired to entertain King Dareall. The tall-as-a-beanpole **Jester Gummoo Hooperbottom** and the short-as-a-sausage-dog-puppy **Jester Humster Pottyworthy**. The jesters would get to work every morning, trying all the tricks and jokes they could think of. The courtiers would enjoy their stupidity, but the Royal family remained stone-faced. Finally, one day the Jesters were warned they would be fired from the job and better Jesters would be brought from the neighbouring kingdom. That day, the jokes and the stories blew all boundaries. This is what happened.

Gummoo Hooperbottom: *What did one plate say to the other?*

Humster Pottyworthy: *Dinner is on me!* (few laughs, King serious)

Humster Pottyworthy: *What kind of a dog does a magician have?*

Gummoo Hooperbottom: *A Labracadabrador!*

(again a few laughs, King serious)

Gummoo Hooperbottom: *How do you make an octopus laugh?*

Humster Pottyworthy: *With ten tickles!*

(few laughs, King starts to look interested)

Humster Pottyworthy: *What do you call an alligator who solves mysteries?*

Gummoo Hooperbottom: *An investigator!*

(many laughs, hint of a smile on the King's face)

Gummoo Hooperbottom: *What's a cat's favourite dessert?*
Humster Pottyworthy: *Chocolate mousse!*

(many more laughs, half-smile on the King's face)

Humster Pottyworthy: *Why can't a leopard hide?*
Gummoo Hooperbottom: *Because he's always spotted!*

(many laughs, King looks eager to hear more)

The courtiers decide to join in

Gummoo Hooperbottom: *Knock, knock*

Courtiers: *Who's there?*
Humster Pottyworthy: *Tank*
Courtiers: *Tank who?*

Gummoo Hooperbottom: *You're welcome!*

(courtiers happy, King looks relaxed)

The excited courtiers decide to continue

Humster Pottyworthy: *Knock, knock.*

Courtiers: *Who's there?*
Gummoo Hooperbottom: *Ice Cream*

Courtiers: *Ice cream who?*

Humster Pottyworthy: *I SCREAM SO YOU CAN HEAR ME*

(court is in splits, the King **SMILES**)

The Queen, Prince and courtiers' joy knows no bounds

They encouraged the Jesters to up their game

Gummoo Hooperbottom: *Knock, knock*

Courtiers: *Who's there?*

Humster Pottyworthy: *Lettuce*

Courtiers: *Lettuce who?*

Gummoo Hooperbottom: *Let us in, it is cold out here!*

(court happy, King is starting to enjoy and keeps SMILING)

Humster Pottyworthy: *Why is Cinderella bad at soccer?*

Gummoo Hooperbottom: *Because she's always running away from the ball!*

(court is happy, and King is smiling away and enjoying)

Gummoo Hooperbottom: *Why did the student eat his homework?*

Humster Pottyworthy: *Because the teacher told him it would be a piece of cake!*

(court is delighted with the result, King has a very broad grin on his face).

The courtiers requested the Jesters to keep going, till the King laughed. It was NOW or NEVER. Very encouraged by their success the court jesters decide to relate a story. This is what they said as everybody listened in pin-drop silence.

*"This is a very scary story. There was once a sly, angry and wicked fox. He hated everything and everybody. He just wanted to destroy everything that came his way. Close to*

*where he lived in his cave in the forest, was a sweet bird. She was always very happy and loved to sing through the day. She lived happily in her nest in the tall oak tree. She was sweet and the fox was grumpy. But the happy bird was not afraid. She had wings and could fly away from the dangerous fox. One day the bird laid some eggs. She would now have to hatch those eggs to get babies. This made her very happy. She loved babies. She started making her nest stronger so it would not be blown away in heavy thunderstorms. She had also started wondering if the fox would be able to harm her babies once they hatched. Meanwhile, the fox too was planning to have babies.* ***So, the fox laid eggs and prepared to hatch them.****"*

There was a wave of giggles across the courtroom. Many burst out in loud guffaws. Fox? laying eggs? to have babies? unheard of!! This was so not possible that it was extremely funny.

Dr. Dano shouted out loud, *"Hey Jesters, foxes don't lay eggs........Hahahaha"*

Jester Gummoo Hooperbottom took not a moment and replied, *"this is OUR story"* and Jester Humster Pottyworthy continued, *"and in OUR story, foxes do lay eggs."* That sounded so hilarious that the courtiers were rolling on the floor laughing, till their stomachs were aching. **The King too started laughing.** A loud roar of laughter filled the room. Everyone went crazy. The task of making the King laugh had been accomplished. It was a day the people of Kola would never forget. Joy and laughter had, after so many years, returned to Kola. However, Zurika was still missing.

King Dareall was recovering fast. His health and mood were both very much better. Seeing this, Prince Nicholas said to the King, "Father, I am now twenty-three years old and would very much like to go in search of our Zurika. Please do give me permission to travel to lands far and wide and search every gypsy camp that ever existed. I am very sure I will find her. I saw her alive in my dream last night and she was waiting to be brought back. Please, please do let me go." The King agreed, provided he promised to return to the palace, in four months, should he not succeed.

A big feast was planned for Prince Nicholas to which everyone in Kola was invited. As the Prince was setting out, the children enacted a goodbye song. They danced and sang to give him a happy send-off and to wish him luck.

*"Wave high, wave low, we think it's time for our Prince to go*

*Wave your elbows, wave your toes, wave your knees and wave your nose*

*Wave your chin, wave your lips and blow a kiss with your fingertips*

*Wave your ears, wave your eyes, wave your hands and say GOODBYE"*

Prince Nicholas left, disguised as **Zangoora the Woodcutter.** Everyone bid him a tearful, but hopeful goodbye. Prince Nicholas, who we will now, call Zangoora, had a plan. He knew exactly where he would go and how to get there. In his dream, he had seen Zurika by the sea.

Things, however, were not as easy as he had imagined. Two months had flown past and Zurika was nowhere to be found. Zangoora had travelled through many gypsy camps living amongst them in dirt and filth.

One night, tired and sad, he slept in the deserted graveyard of an old church. While falling asleep, he was trying to cheer himself up by humming,

*"I will see you somewhere in dreamland, somewhere in dreamland tonight. Over a bridge made of moonbeams, we will find our clouds are silver-lined. Each little star is a castle, shining a welcome so bright. Dreams will come true for me and for you, somewhere in dreamland tonight"*

Zangoora dreamt of Zurika, yet again. She was all grown up and looked as pretty as a picture in gypsy attire. She was calling out to him while waiting by a pretty seaside gypsy camp. Zangoora woke up with a

start. This was surely a message from God that he was very close to finding her. He rushed to the next place, which was **Beyonsea,** the beautiful walled city by the sea. It was a pretty place, much like what he had seen in his dream.

Zangoora just knew he would find Zurika somewhere around there. He had, however, to be careful of not being found out. If the gypsies got to know who he was, he would surely be killed. Rescuing Zurika was going to be difficult. As Zangoora walked around town, he saw many shifty-eyed,

crafty-looking gypsies, whom he avoided. Gypsies have a habit of hiding large folding knives called 'navajos' inside their belts and under their shirts and would randomly stab people.

Zangoora wandered around Beyonsea to find the gypsy camping ground. He chatted with some people around and was told that for the past many years, gypsies had been banned from entering the city.

The gypsies had been shifted to an area beyond the walls of Beyonsea. They could park their caravans there, and were permitted to enter the city limits only very rarely. Once in

Beyonsea, they were always being watched closely. Nobody trusted them.

Eventually, when the sun was about to set, Zangoora chanced upon a gypsy man and befriended him. He had a strange name – **WashingBeard**. Zangoora told him that he was a poor woodcutter from a faraway land, looking to live amongst the gypsies for a few months and earn a living. WashingBeard seemed decent and gentle and agreed to take him along to the camp. What Zangoora saw at the camp was mind-boggling!

The camp had three very distinct divisions. To the right was a very clean, green area where gypsy caravans were parked. Pretty gypsy folk were going about their evening chores and children were playing in the meadow behind.

In the middle was an area where blacksmiths, basket makers and floral garland makers were working.

To the left was a garbage dump, full of trash and filth. Filthy tents were pitched randomly and the place had the most disgusting stench. People there looked like they hadn't bathed for a long time.

As instructed by WashingBeard, Zangoora walked straight to their tent with his head held down. He was relieved to see it was not very dirty. He peeped out and all he could see was filthy people, garbage and trash littered all over. It made him wonder if Zurika could, indeed, be in such a disgusting place.

That night, Zangoora slept fitfully. Early the next morning, he woke up to a melodious song. He hurriedly stepped out into the pile of dirt and was about to rush in the direction of the song, when WashingBeard quickly ran after him and held him back. Zangoora had forgotten the warning he had been given to not go anywhere, until he had first been introduced to the chieftain, who had yet to permit Zangoora to live with them.

Both the song and the voice kept haunting Zangoora. The next morning, he heard the song again. Magic was in the air for Zangoora. He ran to the work area, beyond which, he was not allowed. Standing there, he saw in the meadow an exquisite maiden, singing. Zangoora knew instinctively that he had found Zurika. He just had to get close enough to see if she had a beauty spot on her left cheek. That was her birthmark and her identification. Impatient as he was, he knew he must wait for the right time or he could put both their lives in danger.

Luck favours the brave and the wise. Zangoora got an opportunity sooner than expected. That night, WashingBeard informed him that the genteel gypsies on the other side of their camp had organised a Gypsy Fair. These fairs were much-awaited events and lots of people would attend. The organisers had asked him to help them in setting up stalls. He had given Zangoora's name as a helper too, so that Zangoora could earn some money. This was perfect!

Early next morning Zangoora was ready and eager to get to work beyond the boundaries that had been set for him. Zangoora and his companion helped build and decorate the many colourful stalls and signages.

Whilst resting between jobs, Zangoora's eyes were constantly on the camp. He was observing the lovely maiden he had seen earlier that morning. WashingBeard, on seeing his interest, began familiarising him with the people around. He told Zangoora that the lovely girl sitting on the steps of her caravan was Zurika and the two boys were **Django** and **Otto**. Thereafter, he pointed out **Mama Elspeth**, a charming, kind-looking lady who was the uncrowned queen of the genteel gypsy band. She was by her

caravan, parked very close to Zurika's and was hovering around, keeping a close eye on Zurika. WashingBeard explained that Zurika lived like a Princess and was the apple of Mama Elspeth's eyes. He also pointed out Zurika's best friends

- the very charming **Clementina** – who was a wonderful artist

- elegant **Elvaira**, who did excellent hand embroidery

- lovely **Lolita,** the most graceful dancer of all and

- pretty **Priscilla**, who was an amazing acrobat.

Zangoora could not help but ask about Zurika while trying very hard to hide his excitement. WashingBeard told him that Zurika was like a precious jewel. It was hard to believe she was born a gypsy. In everything she did, she was the best. Zangoora could feel a sense of pride surging through.

WashingBeard continued, by pointing to a cocky-looking girl with a pumpkin in her hand, standing alone and scowling. He warned Zangoora about her. She was the daughter of **Witch Wolfmoon** and Wizard **Walarook** and was evil, crafty, nasty and dangerous. She would play nasty tricks, cast evil spells and harm anyone without any reason. She enjoyed seeing people in pain and distress.

That night, Zangoora went to bed a happy man. He was nearing the end of his hard journey and would soon be home. As it is, this gypsy life had been a rude shock to him. Besides the other inconveniences, the pungent gypsy food was upsetting his stomach. He just could not bear to eat fermented food like sauerkraut any longer. What he loathed most was eating hedgehogs, which was considered a gypsy delicacy. It made him sick! In his contented state, he overslept and woke up to loud music, fun and laughter all around.

Zangoora jumped up, got dressed and ran out. Today was **THE DAY**. His heart was racing as he tried hard to hide his excitement. As he entered the fairground, he spotted Zurika along with her friends, as always - watched over by Mama Elspeth. He must wait to get closer to see the beauty spot on her cheek.

Meanwhile, a group of boys, while performing dangerous gymnastics had lost their balance, toppled down and got injured. Zangoora and WashingBeard rushed to help the boys as did Mama Elspeth. Zangoora, who had quickly scooped up two little boys into his arms, was led by Mama Elspeth to her caravan, for first-aid. An hour into the incident, when all had been treated and certified safe, Zangoora looked up to see Zurika right by his side, patting and consoling one of the young lads. On her

cheek was the beauty spot. Yes! He had indeed found Zurika! How happy he was! Since Mama Elspeth was around, Zangoora decided to befriend her. Elspeth had been very impressed with Zangoora. She knew immediately that he could not be a gypsy. He seemed too well-bred, and well-behaved. To give herself time, to know him better, she offered him some delicious food and drink and sat him down to chat. How grateful Zangoora was for the very delicious meal he had been served! The first good meal since he had left his palace. Mama Elspeth was convinced that he was neither a woodcutter nor a gypsy and that he had some other reason for being there. Zangoora too felt Mama Elspeth was not of gypsy origin and must have a backstory. He wondered why she was so protective of Zurika. What could be the connection? And so, forgetting the fair, both Mama Elspeth and Zangoora settled down for a comfortable chat. After all, they were both curious to know more about each other!

Mama Elspeth told Zangoora how the gypsies had deteriorated as a tribe. Gypsy children on the other side of their camp had never attended school or even done home-schooling. The gypsy women had taken to begging outside churches with stolen children in their arms, to gain sympathy. The gypsy men had ceased working and would make a living from selling stolen goods like saddles and bridles, guns, clothing, tools, horses, flocks of sheep and goats.

There was a famous saying amongst them that *while education promises rewards in the never-never, stealing children, pick-pocketing, home invasions, muggings and contract murder put money in their hands now.* Once known as perfect craftsmen, fortune-tellers and entertainers. they had been welcomed for their skills. Now, they were considered suspicious and dangerous outsiders. Mama Elspeth also explained that she had separated her group and kept them away from all other gypsies. That is why they were so visibly different.

Zurika sat there silently, listening to the discussion. She was feeling uneasy. Seeing Zangoora reminded her of the many flashes she would have in her dreams. She would see palaces, courtiers, guards, soldiers, huge palace grounds, nobility and royalty. She had shared her dream often with Mama Elspeth but Mama would always distract her and ignore the topic. Zangoora felt familiar to Zurika like they had met before and knew each other. This thought both scared and puzzled her. Zangoora, on his part, was very vague in his stories to Mama Elspeth. He had to get to know her better before trusting her with his secret. He must wait a while longer and first earn her trust and confidence. Gradually, since Zurika was sitting by, Zangoora drew her into their conversation asking her about herself. Zurika was shy, soft spoken and gentle. Mama Elspeth left them talking, to go and check on Otto and Django, hoping they had not got into mischief at the fair. Zurika told Zangoora that she was fascinated by magic, witches and wizards, their spells and potions and also their curses and rituals. She used to be frightened by them in the past, but Mama Elspeth had explained to her that these were people with ancient knowledge. They could also be healers, teachers, protectors and guides. Mama had convinced her that they were magical creatures and need not be feared.

Suddenly, Zurika jumped up shouting, "**AnaMarie**, where are you? Appear quickly, I have a surprise for you" and with a flutter of wings and twinkling laughter, a pretty fairy appeared, saying,

*"Presto Chango!*
*I am AnaMarie and I'm a giggle fairy*
*You will know when I am near,*
*just listen - then you'll hear.*
*The sound of gentle giggling,*
*the sound of wings wriggling,*
*It's bound to make you smile,*
*if you listen for a while*

*I pour giggles into your heart and this is just the start"*

"Stop stop stop" interrupted Zurika. "Please AnaMarie, meet our gypsy guest Zangoora. He knows nothing about witches and wizards. I am too scared so will you please take us on a guided tour?"

Their first stop was at Zola's. As soon as **Zola**, the fortune teller saw them approach, she ran out of her tent saying,

*"Let me tell your fortune, just give me your hand. I'll look at your future and what fate has planned. Now, you may think it's foolish, just a guessing game. But let me tell your fortune, listen just the same"*

She pulled Zangoora into the tent but Zurika and AnaMarie pulled him out again. They had so much to show him before the day was done. Zangoora looked bewildered. Moving on, they tiptoed to the tent of the mysterious **Swamp Gypsy**. The tent was empty. They looked around and saw her behind a tree with **Witch BroomHilda** and **Witch SeaHag**. They looked angry and ugly and were mixing an evil potion while chanting and dancing around a boiling cauldron. The scene was very scary.

***"The moon will wax, the moon will wane***
***Now we cast the poison bane***

*All our power and all our might*
*We will bring it out tonight.*
*We trap you forever in this jar*
*Now your luck has disappeared far*
*We cast on you lots and lots of pain*
*Again, again and more yet again!"*

Both Zangoora and Zurika freaked out. They had never witnessed anything like this ever before. AnaMarie sensed their fear and knew she could not show them any more of these rituals. She led them to the main fair area, to relax in the happy surroundings. Fairy AnaMarie, while saying goodbye sprinkled some magic dust on them for protection and disappeared as fast as she had appeared.

That night there were three people, who could not sleep. Mama Elspeth kept awake wondering who Zangoora was. Zurika's mind kept wandering to a big palace with golden steps, running hot water, gold basins, many ladies-in-waiting. Lots of feasting, a kind playmate, ruby rings and chains. Sugary cakes, tiaras and crowns, thrones and courtrooms. A king and a queen, beautiful gowns and spiffy dresses. Zangoora lay awake thinking he would have to take Mama Elspeth into confidence. Without that, there was no way he could take Zurika with him, back to where she belonged.

The next morning, Zangoora had barely woken up when Otto and Django ran in with a message. Mama Elspeth had invited him over to spend the day, on her side of the gypsy camp. Zangoora dressed hurriedly and landed up at Mama Elspeth's caravan.

Without further ado, Zangoora told Mama Elspeth the entire story and how he had succeeded in locating Zurika. Mama Elspeth looked more relieved than surprised. She had hoped and prayed for the day she would send Zurika back to where she belonged. She had forcibly snatched Zurika out of the clutches of the vilest gypsies almost twelve years ago. She had guessed Zurika was of wealthy and aristocratic lineage. For fear of Zurika being harmed by the big bad world, Mama Elspeth had adopted Zurika as her own and protected, educated and taught her all the good things she would be expected to know, were she ever reunited with her birth family.

There was, however, one major worry. It had never been easy for a gypsy to leave his band. **Even if not born a gypsy, once a gypsy, one had to be a gypsy till their dying day**.

Together, Zangoora and Mama Elspeth devised a plan. They would include WashingBeard in their gang and along with Zurika, in the dead of night, escape from the gypsy camp, not stopping till they reached the Kingdom of Kola.

It took a lot of persuasion from Zangoora to get Mama Elspeth to agree to go with them. But, the love for Zurika and the joy of seeing her back in her fold was something Mama Elspeth just could not resist.

Zangoora set out to turn their plan into reality. He confided in WashingBeard and offered him a comfortable and happy life in Kola. The two then readied the horses and hitched them to Mama Elspeth's wagon in the woods behind the meadow.

On a dark, moonless night, Zangoora and WashingBeard sneaked into the woods, along with Mama Elspeth and Zurika. They travelled as fast as they could, stopping only to rest the horses.

Soon, they had safely arrived in the Kingdom of Kola. There was feasting and celebration for many days. King Dareall was the happiest; Queen Iza was delighted to have her children back; the courtiers were proud of their brave Prince Nicholas and delighted to have their gorgeous Zurika among them. The people just could not stop themselves from dancing.

The Kingdom of Kola became a magical place where only happiness, joy, excitement, prosperity and love reigned. Zurika was back home, and they would never stop celebrating her return.

# Sunshine Survives

***A true story of a baby elephant's journey of healing from snare victim to survivor***

This delightful story is set in the beautiful continent of Africa. It is the second-largest continent in the world and has the largest population of wild animals. **Khanyisa** was unlike anything seen before. A tiny albino elephant, with light blue eyes like the ocean and puffy pink cheeks. Albino elephants are very rare – almost white, turning a light pink when wet.

**Khanyisa** was only four months old and had been through much sadness in her life. She had lost her mother, and her herd of relatives, and almost lost her life after being caught and trapped in a poacher's snare.

Poachers are greedy people who illegally kill animals for money. Elephants are hunted for their tusks, which are the two long teeth protruding out from either side of the trunk. These tusks are made of ivory and are very expensive.

**Khanyisa's** mother was robbed of her tusks and killed. **Khanyisa** was left to starve and die of the many injuries she suffered when falling into the deep pit. She was of no use to the poachers since baby elephants grow tusks only after they are two years old.

Our story begins when **Khanyisa** is rescued by Adine Roode and her team. **Khanyisa** (which means SUNSHINE in one of the African languages) was taken to **HERD Elephant Orphanage**. She was seriously injured with a snare around her head, which was cutting into her flesh and bleeding. Her left ear was almost cut off. She also had severe wound injuries around her neck, mouth and cheeks. She had been without food and water for many days and her eyes were swollen and could not open. It was a miracle that she was found alive!

At first, her wounds were treated and cleaned, so no infection would set in. Dr Peter Rogers the wildlife vet, Adine and her carers took turns to make sure that **Khanyisa** was looked after day and night. The poor baby needed special care for her many injuries - her torn, sensitive, pink skin, her ripped apart ear and her hardly-open bright blue eyes. They decided to start operating on her, once she was better and looked stronger.

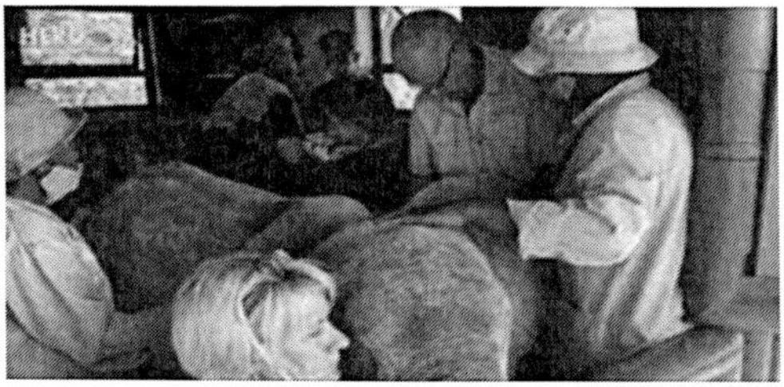

After several operations, over many months, **Khanyisa** was nursed back to health. Because of the many surgeries and partly open wounds, Khanyisa had to wear a blanket vest for protection.

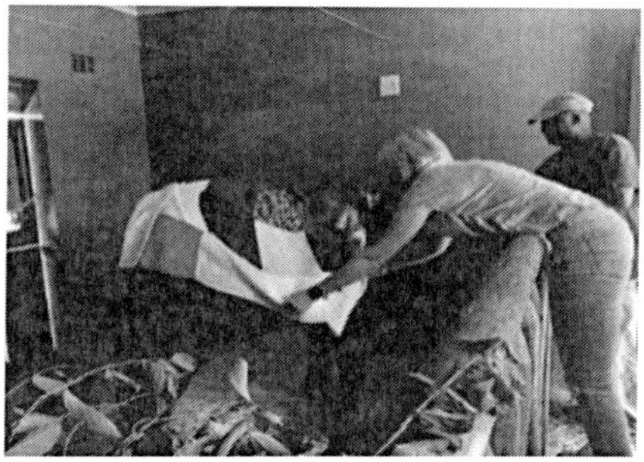

The vest in the picture was knitted by Marcus' animal lover grandmother. Many grannies have sent knitted vests to help protect Khanyisa.

**<u>Would you like to do something like that for other orphaned, injured and sick baby elephants?</u>**

**Enayah, 8 years old, living in Mumbai India – says,** ***"My Nani knits and will make a beautiful, thick, pink blanket and we will send it to Aunty Adine"***

**Alexander, 7 years old, living in Apple Valley, California – says** ***"I would help sick baby elephants who have no mother by finding them some baby elephant friends. Friends always make everyone happy."***

**Ryan, 6 years old, living in Mumbai, India – says** ***"I would like to give apples and bananas from trees to make them better."***

**What do you say?**

**Khanyisa** – who we will, now onwards, call SUNSHINE, was kept in a nursery, separate from the herd.

There, she lived with Lammie the lamb, who was, in time, to become SUNSHINE's best friend. Lammie, the loveable legend is SUNSHINE's ultimate protector and companion.

Lammie also has a woolly companion, Nungu. Lamb Nungu is gentle, patient, sweet and shy. She is also very old. Nungu thoroughly enjoys having SUNSHINE as company but seems quite happy that Lammie has heaps of energy to always play with and keep SUNSHINE entertained. They graze together, chase one another, play and headbutt.

As SUNSHINE was getting stronger and healthier, Adine decided to get her introduced to the other elephants. At first, they would communicate through the fence that divided the nursery from the rest of the orphanage.

Whenever SUNSHINE stepped out, her carers held up an umbrella to protect her delicate skin and healing wounds from the sun.

When it rained, she would be covered by a raincoat.

As time went by, SUNSHINE was getting restless and longed to be with the other elephants. Till that could be possible, her human carers gave her lots of love and attention. She received regular bottle feedings and treats of chunks of sweet potatoes, which she loved!

Blue medicine was applied to her wounds and she was showered with plenty of cuddles and snuggles!

Soon, SUNSHINE was ready to be part of the elephant herd. She was very happy to be able to share their adventures and be part of the action.

Some of the elephants in the herd family are:

**TOKWE** the chief mama elephant and a very confident leader.

**SEBAKWE** the chief papa elephant. He is a gentle giant and very loving and caring towards his herd members.

**LUNDI** is SUNSHINE's adoptive mother and had fallen in love with SUNSHINE as soon as she saw her. Lundi instantly started screaming in joy and excitement. SUNSHINE loves Lundi too and runs straight to her side as soon as she is let out of the nursery.

**TIMISA** and SUNSHINE are like sisters. SUNSHINE gives cheek rubs to Timisa to show her love. They love to wrestle and play together, being almost the same age. Timisa is very scared of the wind.

**KUMBURA** is very sensitive and has an unbelievable bond with SUNSHINE. She is always around her.

**FISHAN** is greedy and possessive about food, which he never shares. He loves being around SUNSHINE and playing with her.

**MAMBO** is the troublemaker and is very naughty. He is, forever, getting into trouble and fighting with the other elephants. The carers cannot let him out of sight even for a minute! But, with SUNSHINE, he is gentle, kind and protective.

**LIMPOPO** limps because of a bone fracture she suffered when she fell into a deep hole made by cruel poachers.

**JABULANI** is a wonderful elephant. He is very inquisitive and can even sniff out a cigarette hiding in someone's pocket!

**Who is your favourite elephant? Why?**

**Enayah, 8 years old, living in Mumbai India – *"Mambo the naughty one. I find him interesting."***

**Alexander, 7 years old, living in Apple Valley, California – *"Sebakwe, because he is gentle and caring and he is the chief papa elephant."***

**Ryan, 6 years old, living in Mumbai, India – *"I like Kumbura because she is big and sensitive."***

**Were you to have a pet elephant, what would you name it?**

**Enayah, 8 years old, living in Mumbai India – says, *"Gajapati"***

**Alexander, 7 years old, living in Apple Valley, California – says *"Ellie"***

**Ryan, 6 years old, living in Mumbai, India – says *"Lemmie"***

**<u>A Day In The Life Of SUNSHINE</u>:** is spent eating, swimming in the waterhole, fighting and playing, mud wallowing, sand bathing, walking, bonding…

SUNSHINE's time out with the herd is invaluable. It is where she learns all the important elephant tricks and talents. Her adoptive mother Lundi, and all her 'aunts' help to care for her. She is the herd favourite.

Mornings come early in the wilderness. The sky is still dark and the stars can be seen twinkling, as the elephant herd gets ready to leave for the bush. After waking up and getting her morning milk bottle, SUNSHINE heads straight to graze outside, in her private garden patch, with her friends and roommates, Lammie and Nungu.

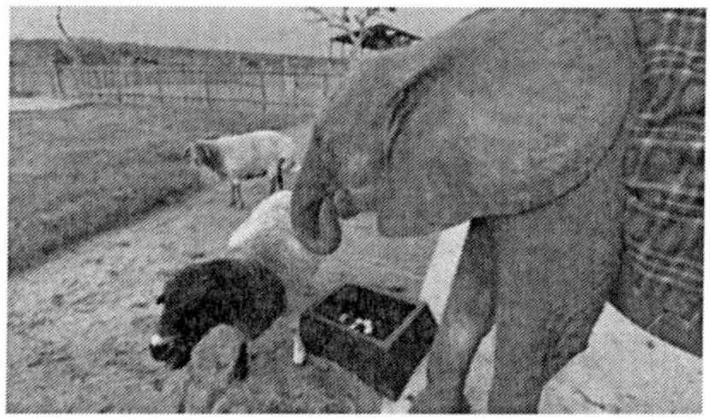

Only after that does she go running to her herd family who are waiting for her.

This is always such a precious scene - like a child heading off to school! The carers are always there, to make sure everyone is safe. SUNSHINE's caregiver carries a backpack which holds milk bottles and a hot water bottle to keep the bottles warm. Also, a first-aid kit, were she to get hurt.

Elephants love eating and so does SUNSHINE. They eat all through the day. They eat about 150 kilos of food every day – that would be around 375 cans of baked beans!!! Roots, barks, all kinds of grass, creepers, herbs, leaves and fruit. **Elephants are vegetarian and don't ever eat other animals.** SUNSHINE has learnt to use her trunk for picking up objects. She has also learnt to strip the bark off trees to eat and is now, strong enough to push down small trees. **For elephants, their trunk replaces the human nose.**

She raises her trunk when excited. She can also use her trunk, to suck up water to drink. Limpopo, SUNSHINE, Timisa and naughty Mambo play together and fight on the mud mounds. They love digging and creating waterholes and laying in them. SUNSHINE keeps stumbling and falling on the soft sand and they all enjoy their rumble-tumble game together.

Once done with the playing, they wash themselves with a swim in the dam. Elephants love water most of all. They piggyback on one another and have lots of fun.

Even as a baby, SUNSHINE loved water. She loved playing in the trough filled with water in her private garden.

Elephants have created their very own sunscreen! After a river or swamp bath, they throw up mud and sand all over themselves, with their trunk, to protect their skin from the hot, burning sun. Clever. Isn't it?

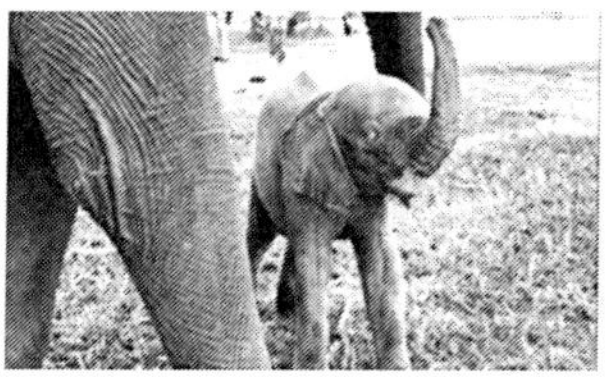

Another favourite game for them is chasing Impalas, who run very fast; baby elephants love chasing them. SUNSHINE enjoys chasing impalas but is confused and scared when she smells hyenas around.

Most animals are scared of elephants, because of their size. Hyenas and crocodiles, however, are known to attack baby elephants. The herd elders and the carers are always attentive, and this has never happened with this herd.

SUNSHINE has slowly learnt all the elephant behaviour and knows the elephant language too! Touching is one of the ways elephants communicate to show they care. Trunk-to-mouth communication is for greeting and bonding, reassuring and comforting. For playing and also making up after a fight.

They console each other in times of stress by 'hugging'

**Would you make this little needy Nelly happy by hugging it?**

**Enayah, 8 years old, living in Mumbai, India – says,** ***"Yes. Why not? Sure!"***

**Alexander, 7 years old, living in Apple Valley, California – says,** ***"I would hug Nelly if she is not muddy and dirty."***

**Ryan, 6 years old, living in Mumbai, India – says,** ***"Yeah. I would love to hug Nelly."***

After a busy day in the bush, with too much playing and running, when SUNSHINE feels tired, she takes a nap while other herd elephants guard her.

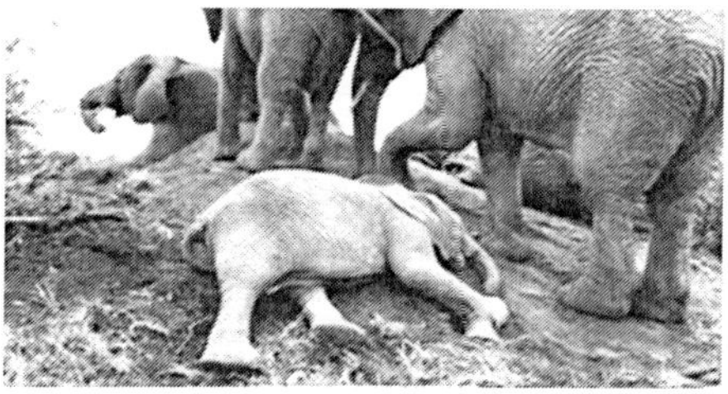

When SUNSHINE and the herd arrive back at sunset, she heads over to the nursery - often with her adoptive mother Lundi, accompanying her to the gate. There, one of the carers welcomes her, with a milk bottle in hand.

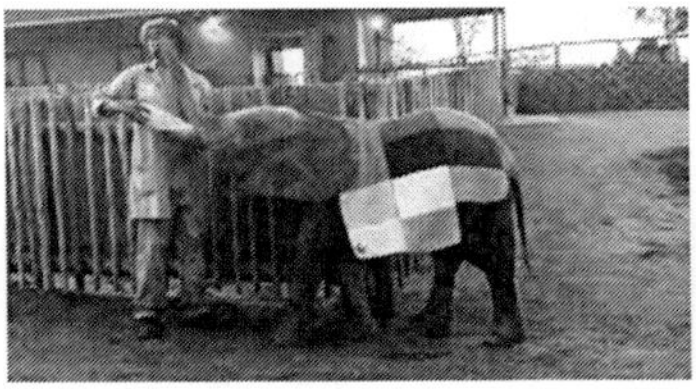 

Having spent the whole day out in the wilderness, SUNSHINE is often ready for bed. Sometimes though, she is still full of energy and plays in the orphanage garden with her tyre tubes.

When it is bedtime SUNSHINE plops down onto her bed of hay, with her carer by her side. SUNSHINE, Lammie and Nungu alternate between sleeping-eating-playing-sleeping-eating-playing through the night. Elephants are restless sleepers and SUNSHINE wakes up for her milk bottle several times. On hot nights, the door is open and she can roam about or sleep outside in her small private garden, where she is promptly joined by her lamb friends.

## HAPPY FIRST BIRTHDAY

Soon, it's celebration time as our brave heart SUNSHINE turns one!! For her 1st birthday on 26$^{th}$ September, 2020, Adine asked all friends and online followers to send Birthday Video Wishes to celebrate the event. Many hundred messages arrived as everyone joined in for a global celebration of love towards one very special albino elephant orphan. OUR VERY OWN SUNSHINE.

**They celebrated her incredible milestone and all it represented: perseverance, tenacity, strength, togetherness, hope and joy!**

**Do you know of anyone who shares SUNSHINE's birthday? Is your birthday on 26$^{th}$ September?**

**Enayah, 8 years old, living in Mumbai India – *her birthday is on 12$^{th}$ March.***

**Alexander, 7 years old, living in Apple Valley, California – *his birthday is on 5$^{th}$ May.***

**Ryan, 6 years old, living in Mumbai, India – *his birthday is on the same date 26$^{th}$ but in a different month, November.***

SUNSHINE continues to grow with her elephant friends, learning the elephant-way-of-life. She looks healthier and stronger and seems braver too. Her confidence and trust have also grown. She has progressed from being a very sick 124 kilos in weight to around 280 kilos!

**<u>Between year 1 and year 2</u>:**

SUNSHINE has learnt that Zebras are harmless and peaceful and will do no harm. So, she walks calmly past them, without feeling scared. It is the Zebras that run away in a different direction, possibly scared of her size!

SUNSHINE has also learnt to be unafraid of buffaloes and now, swims in the dam on the opposite side from where they are.

SUNSHINE is gradually decreasing her milk intake and has started eating pellets, apples and oranges. She simply loves Marulas, which is also Africa's favourite fruit. It is sweet and sour in taste and looks like a yellow plum

  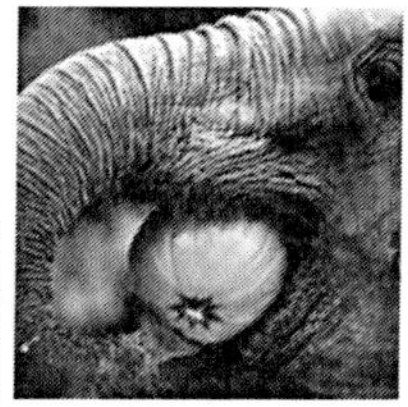

It is said that elephants go mad for marulas and when they eat too many, they get drunk!! Look at the picture below, if you don't believe it!

**SUNSHINE's** grown much naughtier and is always troubling her very patient herd sister Timisa by sitting on her and wrestling with her.

She has by now, learnt to hold her bottle with her trunk.

**Can you guess how much milk Sunshine would drink in a day?**

**Let me tell you – she drinks milk 7 times a day which comes up to a total of 5 litres of milk every single day!**

She has learnt to play soccer (football) and chases the ball round the garden with her human mother Adine, or any carer available to play with her.

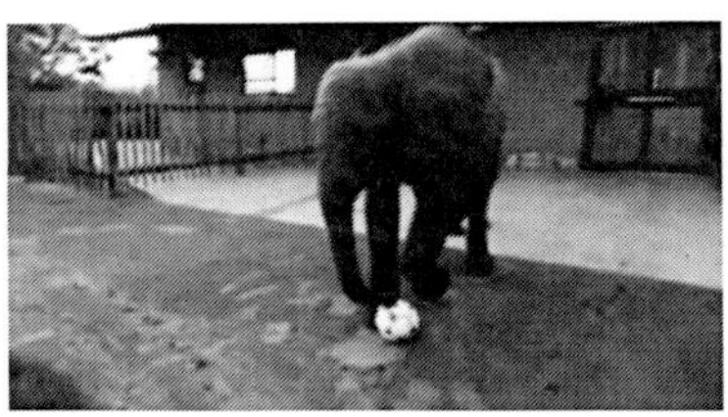

SUNSHINE has turned from being the pinkest elephant in the wild to the muddiest - thanks to all the mud baths she takes!!

You will be sad to know that around this time, SUNSHINE fell very ill, with a stomach infection. Since she was born during covid times, there was very strict lockdown. This delayed her treatment. All her online followers and the orphanage staff prayed hard for her recovery. Fighter that she is, she recovered.

The year flew past.....and soon, it was September once more. The month of celebration when SUNSHINE turned two!!

## HAPPY SECOND BIRTHDAY

Congratulations sweet SUNSHINE! We love your birthday party with your besties, Lammie and Nungu. We love your cake too! Hope you enjoyed your elephant-shaped raw butternut, marulas and sweet potatoes cake!

Adine invited SUNSHINE's followers and donors from around the world to watch the celebration live. She and the carers made an elephant-shaped "cake" for SUNSHINE, with her favourite foods. "Everyone wanted candles and balloons. She is an elephant and we need to respect that. I didn't feel comfortable humanising her birthday," said SUNSHINE's human mother, Adine Roode.

**Can you guess how many people joined in for SUNSHINE's birthday party?**

Close to 7,000 people from around the world attended a virtual birthday party for a rare, albino baby elephant who now weighed a whopping 345 kilos!!

At two years old, SUNSHINE is now extremely intelligent. She and her foster mother, Lundi came across a rhino. And what did SUNSHINE do? She showed no fear, but instead fanned her ears out so that she looked much bigger than she was. **Elephants have extremely large flappy ears.**

When the other herd elephants try to chase hyenas, to keep their young ones safe from harm, SUNSHINE no longer trembles with fear nor does she cry for help. Instead, she observes what the elders do very closely, to be able to copy them later in life. SUNSHINE is very clever at mimicking the elders.

Adine's work, however, is still not done. SUNSHINE must learn to adjust to many changes. She has to move out of her nursery to live with the herd, in their canopy under the stars. For that, she must stop drinking milk at night. She will also need to learn to live like other wild elephants. She will have to overcome the pampering and special treatment given to her by everyone around. This is going to take some time and lots of patience.

There is a rule in the elephant world:

**<u>EVERY ELEPHANT NEEDS A HERD</u> like every child needs a family.**

Our brave little SUNSHINE is no longer a very tiny, ill and scared baby. There is something very peaceful about SUNSHINE. She is full of grace and love.

As SUNSHINE relies less on milk and has started solid food, Adine can let her leave the nursery to live with the herd.

On her last morning at the nursery there are no farewells, no tears, only the joyful gulping down of milk bottles, grassy bites, sheepy comfort and friendly carers!

**Do you think SUNSHINE knew she was shifting out of her nursery?**

**Enayah, 8 years old, living in Mumbai India** –*says, "Yes, I think she knew. She was very keen to join her elephant family and have lots of fun with her friends."*

**Alexander, 7 years old, living in Apple Valley, California** – *says, "I am not sure if she knew about*

***her shifting out of the nursery. I am sure though, she must have been very happy to be with her friends."***

**Ryan, 6 years old, living in Mumbai, India –** ***says, "Yes, she must have known and was excited to go live with the herd."***

When her day in the bush was done, SUNSHINE got back to the gate of her nursery, met Lammie and Nungu, had her last milk bottle for the day and marched right back to the canopy under the stars to have a sleep-over with her friends. She played on the big elephant's sand mound and after that, joined her young friends, in their section of the homestead! Once there, SUNSHINE slowly wound down for the day. She slept and woke up several times in the night, just as she would in her nursery. As the sun rose, SUNSHINE woke up with gusto and soon took to playing with fellow little one, Timisa. All was well.

For Adine and the carers, it was an emotional moment. SUNSHINE had, indeed, passed another test, bravely.

Even as we are all happy at SUNSHINE's story, Adine is sad and worried. She has seen SUNSHINE as a very sick baby who had almost died – grow into a healthy, strong girl. She has seen her shift from the nursery into the homestead - joyfully and comfortably. But this is not the end goal. Adine knows that one day she will need to let SUNSHINE go. **She needs to be a wild elephant again.** She will have to leave the HERD orphanage and be with her own herd of wild elephants, roaming around in the bush. SUNSHINE

would need to learn tough survival skills. As an albino, she will be more visible in the bush and thus, more likely to be attacked by lions, tigers and other big cats. Preparing SUNSHINE for the years ahead will be a difficult task, and the team will now have to take up the challenge to prepare SUNSHINE to live the life she was born to live.

SUNSHINE has not forgotten her woolly friends, Lammie and Nungu. She spends Soulful Sundays with them and also has her last milk bottle by their side, every evening once back from spending her day in the bush… **Elephants are loyal and faithful.** They also have a great memory. **An elephant never forgets!**

Do you know of any fun facts on elephants?

**Enayah, 8 years old, living in Mumbai India – says** ***"In India, we worship Lord Ganesha – Ganapathi, the Elephant God. He brings luck and money, if we pray to Him. When elephants cry, you can see tears."***

**Alexander, 7 years old, living in Apple Valley, California says –** ***"Elephants can't jump. They are afraid of bees. Not one or few bees, but many bees, because they sting and hurt their mouth, eyes and trunk."***

**Ryan, 6 years old, living in Mumbai, India – says,** ***"Elephants are very clever. They can recognise themselves in the mirror! They love bananas and they travel in herds."***

As we move towards the end of SUNSHINE's grand adventure, we must understand why this is such an important story. While all our little readers would have many clever thoughts and ideas about the moral of the story, we also need to understand what it has taught the elders.

It is a story of kindness, care and love towards all creatures big and small, strong and weak. It also tells us that there are some very kind people in the world. They give their time, money and experience to help create a better world. They serve all those who need help. We need more - many more such people.

**Would you like to be one of these people?**

**Enayah, 8 years old, living in Mumbai India – says, *"Yes, of course. My Mumma has taught me that in a world where I can be anything, I must be kind."***

**Alexander, 7 years old, living in Apple Valley, California – says *"Caring is sharing so I would love to be amongst the kind people who will help."***

**Ryan, 6 years old, living in Mumbai, India – says *"Yes, when I grow up I can help the elephants and make them happy."***

**What do you say?**

**Lessons we have all learnt:**

**1. HOPE/POSITIVITY/BRAVERY** - In covid times, when we needed it the most, SUNSHINE gave us hope and joy. She taught all who were scared that by being brave and positive we can win.

**2. ACCEPTANCE/KINDNESS/LOVE** - How one little baby elephant could unite so many people is unbelievable. SUNSHINE, despite being DIFFERENT was loved and looked after by everyone. Nobody shunned her or made fun of her. They were all kind and loving. SUNSHINE continues to shine a light into the world, reminding us to help whomsoever we can, whenever and wherever we can, and to accept one another, whatever our differences.

3. **NEVER GIVE UP/CHOOSE LIFE** - Through all her pain and bad health, SUNSHINE was determined to remain strong, happy and brave and not give up on life.

4. **KEEP THE FAITH/TRUST** - SUNSHINE trusted everyone. She loved everyone. She believed that everyone wanted only the best for her and they were doing their best to help her.

5. **HER SCARS ARE TURNED TO STARS!** She is famous all over the world. Her online followers, love her and follow her story very closely. Her pain has now turned to gain and given her so much fame. She has become a living example of inspirational living.

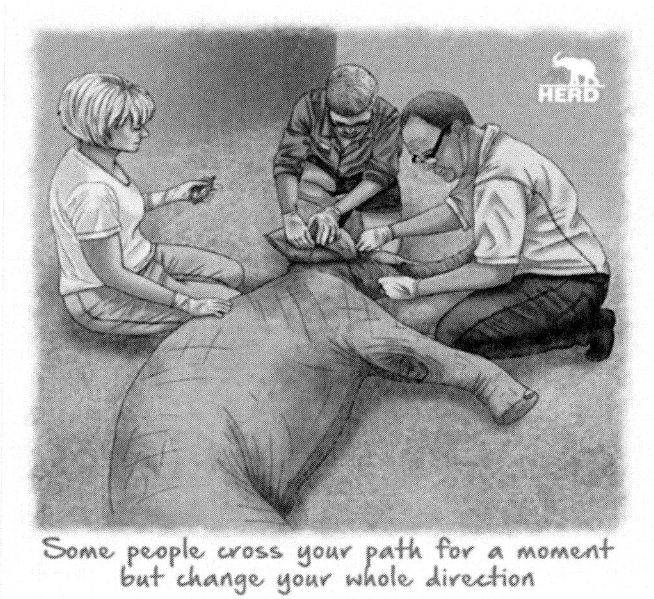

**Has SUNSHINE inspired you? Would you like to meet her?**

**Would you like to spend some nights at a safari lodge, close to all these wonderful elephants?**

**Enayah, 8 years old, living in Mumbai India –says, *"I would love to visit South Africa and meet with all the elephants and see other wild animals.* SUNSHINE *is a truly remarkable elephant."***

**Alexander, 7 years old, living in Apple Valley, California says, *"I think it would be a good holiday plan. I would love to visit* SUNSHINE's *world."***

**Ryan, 6 years old, living in Mumbai, India – *"I would love to go on an evening Safari to see the elephants."***

**Should your answer be "yes", then have your mama check out Jabulani Safari - in South Africa.** https://jabulanisafari.com.

Owned by SUNSHINE's human mother Adine Roode and you could go there for a safari adventure vacation

SUNSHINE's miraculous recovery at HERD, (Hoedspruit Elephant Rehabilitation & Development), South Africa's first dedicated elephant orphanage, has been one everyone will remember forever. Scores of people have watched SUNSHINE's journey online and supported

Adine and her team through SUNSHINE's pain and progress. They have prayed for her recovery in times of bad health and supported Adine through sending donations so that Adine could manage to look after SUNSHINE in the best possible way.

**Would you like to help and support Adine Roode? Would you like to be part of this very noble cause? If yes, then maybe you could join in as donors or adopt an elephant.**

HERD relies on public funding to cover the very high costs of running and maintaining the orphanage and the staff. Raising a baby elephant is very different to raising other animals. Elephants are incredibly complex and sensitive and very expensive to look after.

This is what Sunshine looks like as we end this story. She now weighs 700 kilos.

Who is your most favourite character in this story? WHY?

**Enayah, 8 years old, living in Mumbai India – *"I Love* SUNSHINE. *She is so brave. I also love aunty Adine for her kindness"***

**Alexander, 7 years old, living in Apple Valley, California – *"This is* SUNSHINE's *story. She is the main character and is my favourite too. I am so happy that she did not die."***

**Ryan, 6 years old, living in Mumbai, India - *"My favourite is* SUNSHINE, *the elephant. I love her because she is so happy and friendly."***

## Organization Information

## Hoedspruit Elephant Rehabilitation & Development

LOCATION: Pretoria, Gauteng - South Africa
WEBSITE: **https://herd.org.za**
FACEBOOK: **Facebook Page**
TWITTER: **@HERD_Elephants**
PROJECT LEADER:

**Adine Roode**
Pretoria, Gauteng South Africa

# Chocolate Chocolate Everywhere...And Every Bite To Eat!

Normally, stories begin with **once upon a time**, but this one won't.

Why? .......because this is an unusual story about an amazing little girl, who has a delightful, unreal and amazing adventure.

The story begins with this eight year old girl, sitting by a huge bay-window in her bedroom on the $33^{rd}$ floor of a tall building, overlooking an extremely busy street. It is dusk and she is tired from school, homework and play. She has been there for the longest time, looking at the tiny blinking lights of the cars lined up and moving, in the street very far below, taking people back home from work.

She is wondering whether she should wait for her Mumma to get back home from her studio or go to bed, considering the roads are so very crowded.

Suddenly......she finds herself on a beautiful street with lovely houses... She is delighted and curious as she happily skips along the beautiful tree-lined street to stop at the prettiest and most unusual house. She looks around, and finding nothing familiar, walks straight to the gate of the enchanted cottage. She tiptoes to open the gate and steps right into a delightful garden. She pauses briefly to see the beautiful candy house made from what looked like, the prettiest pink and white candy and brown chocolate. Amazing!! Even the door looked carved from white chocolate with pink trimmings. The garden was full of what seemed like lollipop trees and marzipan and candy flowers. PERFECT.

Happily, she runs to the door– WAIT! She pauses, thinking to herself, 'could this be Hansel and Gretel's home?' and tut-tuts the thought, telling herself, 'can't be. They are just characters in a fairy tale. I am a big girl now and don't take fairy tales seriously.' She testily pushes open the door and hears a cheerful, soothing voice call out, "***Qui est là?*** **(Who is it?)**"

The little girl responds, ***"Excuse me but I don't know what you say!"***

A man comes hurriedly towards her saying," ***Bonjour petite fille*** **(good morning little girl)."**

She frowns. On seeing the tall, handsome man and says, ***"Who are you and why do you speak in a language I cannot understand?"***

The man flashes her a charming smile and politely replies - this time in English, ***"I am sorry dear child. I do very much hope you can understand my English. My name is Oscar Monet Gaker and I welcome you to Paris Incroyable."***

***"Paris what?"*** questions the little girl.

***"Oh, sorry. Amazing Paris, famous world over for the Eiffel Tower,"*** beams the man.

*"Thank you, Sir. I come from Incredible India, the land of the wonderful Taj Mahal"* says the little girl.

***"Welcome again, child. What is your name? How may I help you?"*** asks the man.

*"My name is Enay......oops! My Mumma says never share your name with a stranger. So please, could you call me Missy?"* stutters the little girl.

***"That's smart jolie mademoiselle! I mean pretty girl. And would you like to tell me why you chose Missy as your other name?"*** asks the man.

*"Ooh... you ask too many questions. Sorry I have forgotten your name. It's too complicated,"* says the little girl.

***"They call me Oscar Monet Gaker. And you could call me OMG for short"*** the man responds.

*"OMG? I have a masi back home who says it all the time. I asked her what it means and she said it's the short form for <u>Oh My God.</u> I'd rather call you <u>Mister Master Magicmaker</u>. There's something so magical about this place! My Nani calls me Missy when we are pretend playing. You could call me by that name too,"* the girl proudly responds.

***"Masi? Nani? Could you please explain, jolie mademoiselle"*** requests the puzzled man.

*"Sure. Masi is mother's sister and Nani is mother's mother – so that makes her my grandmother. And, talking of grandmothers, do you know my grandmother?"* asks the little girl.

*"No, I don't but I'd love to! Why do you ask?"* questions the man.

*"Because my grandmother calls me mademoiselle in pretend play when she pretends to be talking to someone grownup,"* explains the girl.

*"That's' clever! So, your... err ...Nani knows French, I presume?"* asks the man.

*"Possible. My Nani knows many things. She is also ....hmmm...a wordsmith,"* says the girl, proudly.

*"That's so clever! How do you know such a big word?"* asks the man, looking very impressed.

*"My Mumma taught me. She says, one who works with gold is called a goldsmith, so one who works with words should be a wordsmith. Simple, isn't it?"* answers the little girl.

*"And what does your Nani do with words?"* asks the man who is very interested in all that the little girl is saying.

*"She is a wizard with words. She does magic with them. You give her any word and she will build a*

*whole story and sometimes, a very comical rhyme around it. It is all very interesting. All my friends love to spend time with her"* says the girl, proudly.

*"And you mentioned err…."* fumbles the man.

*"Masi, my mother's sister?"* reminds the little girl.

*"Yes, yes, that's the one. What does she do?"* asks the man.

*"She's a fabulous chef and she can cook up any meal in a jiffy. And a fancy one at that!"* the little girl replies feeling very proud indeed!

*"Hmmm. I must say, you have a very talented family!"* replies the man who is really impressed. He adds, *"tell me, what brings you here?"*

*'What brings me here? Seriously!! How did I get here? '* wonders the confused little girl.

*"This is Paris Missy, the capital of France. And you just walked in unannounced,"* the man reminds the little girl.

*"Oh! That is rather rude of me! I am sorry. I am eight years old and don't have a clue about how I got here. I chose your house because it is the prettiest one on the street. Which brings me to: why, Mister Master Magicmaker, do you have lollipop*

*trees, candy and peppermint flowers and an edible white chocolate door?"* asks the little girl.

*"Missy, I am a French pastry chef. I work with chocolate and confectionery and am known for my chocolate sculptures. I have also been described by my many admirers as a chocolate architect, a pastry artist and a food painter."* It is now the man's turn to feel proud.

*"OMG! Then, the name Mister Master Magicmaker would suit you perfectly - since you appear to be a famous person, with many admirers!!"* exclaims the little girl.

*"Thank you, Missy. Now that you are here, would you like me to offer you a meal and a tour of my home? Surely, you should be very tired. And would you need, first, to freshen up and then, have some refreshments, before you head back to where you came from?"* suggests the man.

Missy is feeling fuzzy in the head and is clearly confused. Back home? Alone? However, she decides to enjoy the moment. Everything around is so interesting and beautiful.

*"So, Missy, where do you suggest we start from?"* asks the man.

***"Let's start at the very beginning. It's a very good place to start. Do you know The Sound of Music? That's such a lovely song!"*** exclaims the little girl.

***"Hahaha yeah. So let me first take you to the powder room to freshen up"*** suggests the man.

Saying that, he opens a door and Missy steps in, shutting the door behind her. She lets out a loud shriek and rushes right out. The entire room is made of chocolate - from the wash basin, towels, taps and flush to the soap and lights. ***"I can't possibly use a room made of chocolate! Don't you have a normal powder room?"*** asks the agitated little girl.

***"Gotcha,"*** laughs OMG, ***"just kidding. Follow me"*** and she is led into another room. Missy was now ready for some food and, of course, some more surprises and exciting experiences.

OMG leads her into the foyer and says, ***"Since we start at the very beginning, we shall start from here. Missy do please look up at the*** CHANDELIER."

***"Golly! It is gorgeous. Looks so real. Unbelievable!!***

*"This is chocolate art – made from real milk and chocolate and the entire thing is edible. Do you understand edible?"*

*"Yes,"* says Missy. *"It means the entire chandelier can be eaten. Wow. How cool is that!!"*

She then sees the COUCH placed there and is flabbergasted! Chocolate, chocolate and then, some more. *"Boo-yah,'* she exclaims in excitement! *"All made of chocolate, I'm sure!"*

OMG nods a yes, saying, *"Thank you, Missy. Now let us move on. We will visit my studio, my exhibit room and my laboratory. The studio is where I create all the wonderful designs, to present as chocolate art to the world. The exhibit room is where I keep my best and most unique work of art and all-time favourites. The laboratory is where I experiment with various ingredients, which are trade secrets. Hence, I cannot talk much on them."*

*"I have a question"* says Missy. *"OH NO, I have many questions."*

*"It would be my pleasure to answer them, but let us talk while we walk towards the kitchen. I think you*

***will agree that both of us could do with some food."*** suggests OMG.

***"Hurrah, food–glorious food! I am starving,"*** says Missy. ***"Let's go. The questions can wait."***

Off they go the kitchen. What a kitchen!!! Missy is dumbstruck. She tries hard not to let out a yippee!!

***"Missy, my girl,"*** says OMG, with a twinkle in his eye, like he has a mischievous plan up his sleeve. ***"What may I offer you to drink? Tea, coffee, milkshake or fruit juice, besides, of course, some plain water?"***

***"Mister Master Magicmaker. My Mumma frowns when I ask for tea. She says coffee is not good for children. So please may I have a chocolate milkshake, since you have a chocolate factory? And, of course, water before that. Thank you"*** says Missy, feeling very proud for having obeyed her mother.

***"Sure. Here we go"*****.....** and OMG hands Missy a glass of the most delicious looking CHOCOLATE SHAKE ever, along with some water. He pours himself some tea from – HOLY MOLY – a TEAPOT made of chocolate into a chocolate TEACUP. Seemed like she was in chocolate wonderland! Missy rubs her eyes in

sheer disbelief, while OMG pushes a few chocolate CROISSANTS her way.

***"Yummy yummy, rumble tumble in my tummy"*** says Missy, reaching out for the goodies. She gulps down the chocolate shake and gobbles up the croissants. Her mouth, now, feels too sweet! ***"Mister Master Magicmaker, please may I have something that's not sweet?"*** Missy requests.

***"Certainly. What would you like?"*** asks OMG with a mischievous smirk on his face.

***"Fruit?"*** suggests Missy.

OMG hurriedly brings in a whole lot of fruit, while chuckling to himself. ***"Lovely*** CHERRIES; ***luscious*** APPLES; ***sweet*** PINEAPPLE; ***tangy, tempting*** ORANGE WEDGES; ***delicious*** MANGOES. ***All for you"*** offers OMG.

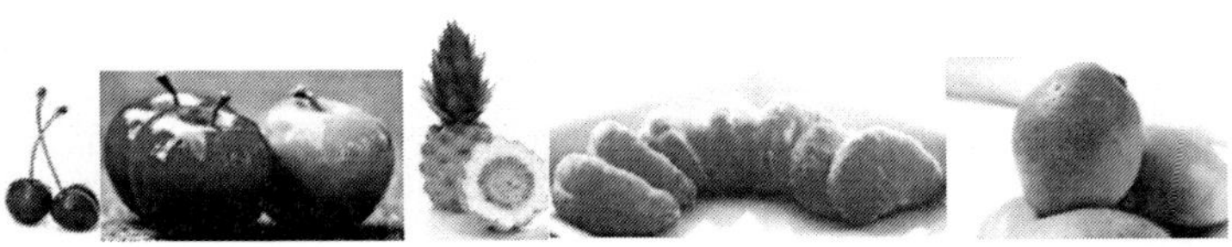

Missy was thrilled. ***"Wow! I love cherries"*** – and so saying picked one up and bit into it. ***"OMG! This looks so real and is made of chocolate!"*** The same was the case with the apples, pineapple and orange wedges. All looked so real and tempting, but were made of chocolate with different stuffing inside. Then, Missy saw the mangoes and went, *"Slurp slurp Mangoes!! My favourite fruit. And, they most certainly look real!"* One bite, and she realised OMG had fooled her yet again. *"Mister Master Magicmaker, I'm not allowed so much sweet. It is bad for the teeth. I am so wanting something not sweet. Would that be - salty?"* wonders Missy.

***"Yes, you could say that. Perhaps, savoury would be a better word. I see that you speak in rhymes, Missy. Your speech is rather lyrical. How come?"***

While Missy is thinking of a reply, OMG reaches out for some REAL FRUIT TARTS, a REAL FRUIT ELEPHANT, some APPLE CINNAMON SAVOURIES and a ready-to-eat CARVED PINEAPPLE.

Some well-crafted kiddy SANDWICHES too.

Missy is completely floored by the looks and presentation of all that was put before her. She would never have imagined that food could look soooo good! She tries her best to eat like a lady – small mouthfuls, dainty bites, no talking whilst her mouth is full – everything her Mumma had taught her. OMG sat by, watching her with amusement as she enjoyed her meal.

***"Let's now head to the Studio. It is my main workplace, where all my creative ideas are used to make beautiful, life-like images."*** says OMG while Missy scurries behind him.

***"Tah-da,"*** says OMG as he opens the door leading to a huge hall. ***"Welcome to my Studio, Missy. Let's head for the Christmas section."***

*"Jeeze the wheeze"* Missy cannot control her excitement. *"This is chocolate heaven! Please may I say something, before we start exploring all the chocolicious delights?"*

OMG guffawed out loud, ***"Certainly. I am all ears."***

*"What does what you just said, mean? Never heard that one before,"* says Missy.

***"It means that I am listening carefully and with full attention. Carry on with what you want to say,"*** explains OMG.

*"Thank you, Mister Master Magicmaker. My Mumma works out of a studio too. It is a bit different, though.*

*No chocolates - only many clothes and a few mannequins. Many lovely ladies, making lots of noise and everyone enjoying while working,"* describes Missy.

*"What does your Mumma do? Is she a dressmaker?"* asks OMG.

*"No. She is a fashion stylist. She creates fashionable looks for the rich and famous. She is up-to-date on latest designs and helps put a beautiful look together. She's very creative – an artist…ahem… maybe, just like yourself?"* says Missy with a twinkle in her eyes and a glow on her face. She always has a glow-up when she remembers or speaks about her Mumma.

*"Ooh la la! That is such a cool thing to do! No wonder you are so proud of your Mumma! Please convey my congratulations to her."* Chatting away, he leads Missy to his CELEBRATING CHRISTMAS section.

*"Golly Ghost,"* says Missy as she looks around, at the CHRISTMAS TREES, SANTA CLAUS, and REINDEER RUDOLF, CHRISTMAS STOCKING stuffed to the brim, in the midst of many PRESENTS and SANTA's BEAUTIFUL HOUSE on the north pole.

Next came the **CHILDRENS' CORNER**. And what a treat it was!!

***"Funsies, funsies,"*** says Missy as she gapes in astonishment at the CAROUSEL, the FERRIS WHEEL, the ROCKING HORSE and the BANDANA BOY. So very beautiful and real!

Next one up was **FASHION FOCUS**. The thought itself was sooo exciting... Missy loved fashion and found her Mumma's work fascinating.

In an absolute frenzy, Missy rattled on.... fast and furious, ***"Oh, how I wish my mumma was here! That's a beautiful*** DRESS! PERFUME......***smells heavenly! What elegant*** SHOES!

*Aha! Don't miss these wonderful, fancy* BAGS!! *How I wish I could take everything for my Mumma"* laments Missy.

OMG smiled a knowing smile as he proceeded to ....

**MUSIC & MELODY** ♫ ♫ ♫

*"Yipee ki-yay!"* goes *Missy, "so much music! SOOOOO GOOD! Please Mister Master Musicmaker, do explain a few of them to me. You see, I don't know much about musical instruments. Except for the piano that I play and the guitar which I'd very much like to learn to play."*

*"This is a* GUITAR. *A string instrument. Played by plucking the six plastic strings either with the fingers or fingernails. You would be very happy to know that the guitar is derived from an earlier instrument found in and around India. It is called the SITAR!"*

*"Hip-hip-hurray, India is the best,"* says Missy, while dancing around the room.

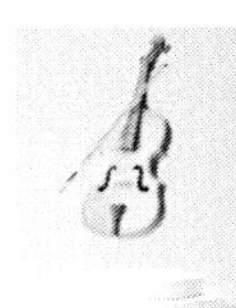

Beaming a smile, OMG moved on to the VIOLIN. *"It is from the Guitar family, but much smaller than the Guitar. It is made from different material, and is played with a bow.*

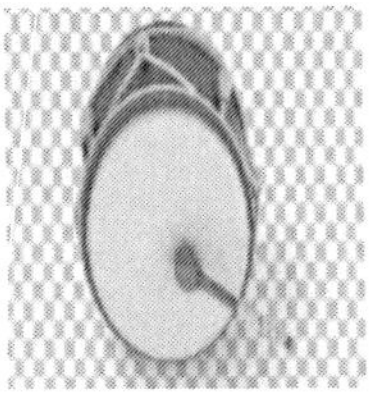

*Coming to the* DRUM. *It"* Missy interrupts, *"Sorry, please may we skip the drum? I am very familiar with drums. What's this funnily-shaped folded piano-like instrument?"*

*"That is an* ACCORDION. *A beautiful instrument invented in Germany. Since it is hand-held when played, it is also known as a known as a Hand Harmonica.*

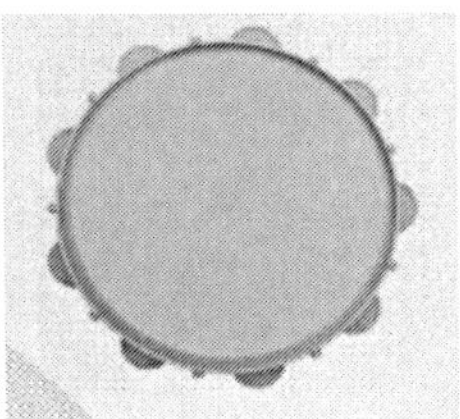

*Look here! This lovely instrument is a* TAMBOURINE. *It has a round frame with many pairs of small metal jingles. It is one of the easiest musical instruments to play.*

*The PIANO"* Missy interrupts yet again… *"May we please skip the piano and move on?"*

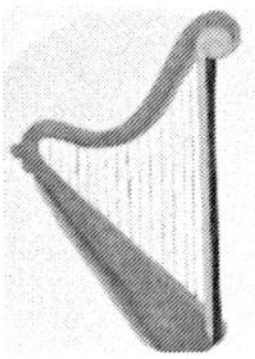

*"Oui jeune fille intelligente* **(yes, clever little girl)**. *This is a* HARP. *Perhaps, one of the oldest musical instruments in the world."*

*"Oh I know that one! It is played by mermaids sitting on a rock,"* explains Missy.

OMG is mighty impressed. He does not know much about these things. He makes a mental note and says, ***"Missy, my next creation will be a mermaid with a harp."***

*"Thank you, thank you, thank you,"* says Missy with a deep curtsy, like her ballet teacher has taught her. She could not help but feel most important!

***"Moving on… to the last two. Both belong to a time much before you were born, and could be called antiques. Only very lucky kids would have seen them in real life. The*** TRANSISTOR RADIO – ***which you could carry anywhere while it plays songs, music or even gives you the latest news. It came before what we now call electronic devices. Like your laptop, cellphone, ipad, all of which I am sure, you are very familiar with. Transistor radios are still commonly used as car radios,"*** describes OMG.

*"Oh! I am a lucky one, then! My great-grandmother has a transistor radio by her bedside,"* says Missy.

*"This one here is a* GRAMAPHONE. *It is an old fashioned record player, from where you could listen to music of your choice, in the olden days."*

*"Why do you make old things which, most of us may never have seen or known of?"* questions a puzzled Missy.

*"Because OLD IS GOLD!! Have you heard that saying before?"* asks OMG.

*"Yes, of course! I have. I thought that saying was for my great grandmother and my nani. They are precious, because they are old."*

*"You are a remarkable little girl, Missy. So intelligent and witty,"* laughs OMG.

*"I am creative too, Mister Master Magicmaker!"* pouts Missy. *"My Nani says WHEN INTELLIGENCE MEETS CREATIVITY, A GENIUS IS BORN. CREATIVITY IS INTELLIGENCE HAVING FUN. Do you agree?"*

*"Quelle fille exceptionnelle,"* (what an exceptional girl!) OMG mutters under his breath.

*"Excuse me!"* retorts Missy.

***"Oh, nothing,"*** replies OMG as he scurries off to the chocolate sculptured, **ANIMAL DISPLAY** section.

Missy follows him. One look and she retraces a few steps in fear.

***"Oh no! This is so spooky! The dragon, the lion and the crocodile look almost real! The gorilla is ferocious. OMG, this is really scary."***

OMG laughs and says, ***"The** DRAGON **is six fee tall and its eyes glow in the dark.***

***The** LION **took five days to craft, with the mane alone taking four hours.***

***Sculpting the scales of the** CROCODILE **was extremely difficult.***

***For the** GORILLA, **I used up forty-five kilos of milk and dark chocolate."***

Moving on, Missy let out a scream, ***"Eeks! look at that elephant, the giraffe and the uhhhh."***

***"King Cobra,"*** says OMG, helping her out.

***"Making the*** ELEPHANT ***was tough, since it is so large.***

***The*** GIRAFFE ***is one my bigger chocolate creations. It is made of 100% chocolate and weighs seventy-two kilos.***

***The*** KING COBRA ***weighs thirty-six kilos."***

***"Why do you have so few animals? The animal kingdom is really vast"*** asks a puzzled Missy.

OMG laughs and says, ***"Yes, I do have some more but I've placed them separately in the*** MUMMIES with BABIES ***section. Come, let's go."***

***"Va-va-voom,"*** shrieks Missy in excitement, ***"this is fantabulous! So cute....simply adorable!"***

OMG took the lead saying, ***"this section melts my heart, while I melt chocolate to make them. The*** SEA TURTLE ***with the*** BABY ***on its back is all love. It took me four days to complete and is,***

*perhaps, the warmest depiction of the love between a mother and its baby.*

*The* CHAMELEON *with its* BABY *riding on its back is so realistic. It shows the trust babies have in their mothers –* DO NOT FEAR WHEN I AM NEAR, *the mothers seem to say.*

*The* FOX *and the* FOXPUP *are my personal favourite.*

*If you will notice, the* TIGER *and its* CUB *is a life-size sculpture.*

*Just see this cuteness overload! The* KANGAROO *and the little* JOEY *in the pouch."*

Missy, overcome with emotion, and missing her Mumma, wants to cry. She quickly regains her composure and says, *"A mother is your first friend, your best friend and your forever friend."*

Before OMG could ask her why she was tearing up, smart and brave Missy laughed and blew kisses towards the exhibits. She says, *"Mwah mwah to all the babies. They are so adorable. Mister Master Magicmaker, you need to add to your animal collection. Have you no birds or sea creatures?"*

***"Brilliant observation,"*** says OMG looking very impressed. ***"Yes, I do have a few. I've recently lent them out for display in a chocolate museum in Zurich, which is in Switzerland."***

Missy promptly jumps in saying, *"Oh Switzerland! That is where I hope to go skiing. I, very recently, learnt skiing in Gulmarg, which is in Kashmir. It is, perhaps, the prettiest place in India. After I am done with my course in Gulmarg, I shall be a certified skier. Isn't that great?"*

OMG looks even more impressed. ***"That's super! You are such a talented, multi-faceted girl!"***

Missy smiles and replies, rather officiously, *"Thank you. Now, if you would be kind enough to give me some paper and a pencil, I would like to leave a few suggestions for your next projects."*

With the naughtiest twinkle in his eye, OMG rushes to get paper and pencil and hands it over. *"Now tell me. Have you made a sea-horse?"* asks Missy, to which OMG nods a 'no'. Missy stares in disbelief as she starts to write. Only to realise that the book was made of chocolate and the pencil….

OMG guffaws loudly saying, ***"fooled you yet again, Missy. The*** WRITING BOOK ***is made of chocolate. The*** PENCIL ***is lemon pie in disguise, with crunchy chocolate and lemon mousse. The*** ERASER ***is made of pink lemonade marshmallow."***

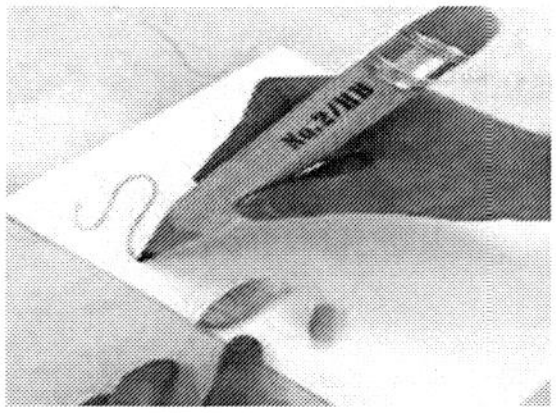


Missy smiles back cutely, ***"Would you please be kind enough to write? My (ahem) spellings are not too good, yet."***

OMG getting out his pen and writing pad says, ***"Certainly, Missy. With pleasure. I will take down your orders and work on them."***

Missy nodded saying, ***"Starting from the beginning, you could add some*** BELLS ***and a*** MISTLETOE, ***some glittery*** CANDLES ***and*** STOCKINGS ***to your*** CHRISTMAS COLLECTION. ***For the*** ANIMAL COLLECTION. ***you definitely need a pretty*** PUPPY ***named OREO, a*** PANDA ***named POLLY, a*** PENGUIN ***named PENNY and a*** DOLPHIN ***named DESTINY."***

OMG nodded seriously as he walked towards the next section while taking notes. *"This is the* FLIGHT & FEATHERS *section,"* he says. *"The one with a branch is a* DOVE. *Doves are symbols for love, purity, hope and most importantly peace. This is a very meaningful exhibit in these times of war and unrest."*

*"Yes indeed!"* Missy solemnly agrees, *"very pretty too."*

*"The next one is a* BALD EAGLE *and it is the national bird of the United States of America."*

*"Not fair"*, says Missy, sounding very offended. *"How come the national bird of India, the* PEACOCK, *is not here? Please do add one to your list Mister Master Magicmaker. Thank you."*

*"Whoopsie, that's a serious error Missy. Will make one soon"* promises OMG. *"This lovely bird you may never have heard of, is a* PHOENIX. *It is an immortal bird. It does not die. It burns in a show of flames, and then comes back to life by rising from its own ashes. This one was extremely difficult to*

*make. It took me five days. Hand-crafting the many chocolate feathers took forever!*

*And, do you see the lovely* CAGE?*"*

Missy looking sad says, *"I don't like cages. They are cruel. My Mumma says birds are born to be free and fly high in the sky. It is cruel to lock them in cages, however pretty the cage may be."*

OMG nodded in agreement. *"Very true, Missy. I made this on the insistence of my bird-loving nephew. If you notice, I have put the birds outside the cage and not in it.*

*Now to the last exhibit in this section – the* WHITE SWANS *and the* BLACK SWANS. *They are so graceful and elegant as they glide on the water….it's been a true pleasure to craft them."*

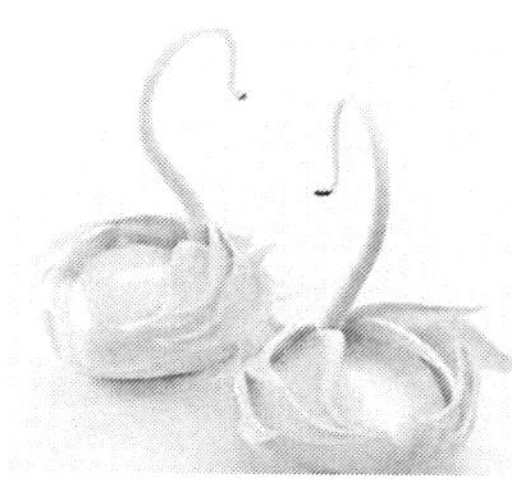

Interrupting OMG, Missy pipes in *"My Nani says, A THING OF BEAUTY IS A JOY FOREVER. Let me tell you an interesting story about swans. I can't guarantee if it is completely true, though."*

***"Yet another story?"*** laughs OMG**,** ***"Okie dokie, please do tell me."***

Taking a deep breath, Missy starts her little speech, *"Her Majesty the Queen owns all the swans in Britain and only she is allowed to eat them. Ordinary people must only see them gliding on water. White swans could be owned by other companies as allowed by the Queen. Black swans, however, are owned solely by Her Majesty. Sadly, because the beautiful and gracious Queen Elizabeth is now dead, King Charles III is their new owner."*

OMG now walk towards the **SPORTS AND BOARD GAMES** section.

*"Wish I knew how to ride bikes and drive cars! I can barely manage my bicycle,"* laments Missy.

***"Time yet for driving. You have to be eighteen years old. The race car took six days to make and***

***consumed a lot of chocolate,"*** says OMG moving to the BOARD GAMES. ***"The*** CHESS BOARD ***is made of dark and white chocolate. A delicious pistachio and raspberry cake has been disguised as the*** DARTBOARD. ***You get to eat the slice your dart lands on.***

***The*** FOOTBALL ***is every child's dream project. As also the*** SKATEBOARD. ***The*** DUMBELLS ***are for use after having eaten too many chocolates,"*** jokes OMG.

Suddenly, he realises that Missy has been unusually quiet and turns around to see her yawning. ***"Tired is it?"*** asks OMG while patting her gently on the head. ***"Now, what you are about to see will wake you up."*** So saying,

OMG drew the curtain open to reveal the hidden treasure. ***"This is my* ROYALTY *section."***

***"Ole!" this is a winner!"*** Missy danced around in joy. ***"How I wish I could present these treasures to King Charles III, at his coronation next week. Do you think he would agree to wear this beautiful*** CROWN ***and invite me to his coronation? Please, please let me take these; I so want to attend the regal event!"***

OMG readily agrees. ***"Possible little girl. I have been invited as the Pastry Master Chef at the coronation dinner. Perhaps, we could meet at the royal banquet. Wouldn't that be awesome?"***

Glancing outside the window, OMG observes, ***"It is getting rather late and the sun is about to go down. Besides, you have a long way to go Missy, so let us rush to my LABORATORY to see what I consider my best, most difficult and unusual creations."***

*"A Laboratory?"* interrupts Missy, *"I would like to become a scientist when I grow up. For that, I will have to do all my research in a laboratory. It will be my place of work. But, you are an artist. Why would you need a laboratory?"*

OMG explains, *"Not only scientists and researchers use a laboratory. I, as an artist, use a laboratory as a place where I experiment with my ingredients - to create different shapes and forms in chocolate. It also houses all my tools and equipment. Here we are....*

*The* CHOCOLATE SHARK *is a masterpiece and is one of my largest creation.*

*The chocolate* TELESCOPE *amazed people when they first saw it. It has so much detail and looks so real, nobody was ready to believe it was made from chocolate!*

*Coming to the* STATUE OF LIBERTY, *which is on Liberty Island, in New York (U.S.A.). It is a gift of friendship from the people of France to the people of America. I*

*am a proud Parisian, so I was extremely happy to make this tall chocolate statue, which is my highest work yet.*

*As a tribute to the world of Artificial Intelligence (AI), it is with great pride that I present to you the Chocolate* ROBOT, *the future of our world.*

*And last, but definitely not the least, the chocolate* ROBOT CHEF, *my new helper in the kitchen, who is extremely dear to me."*

Noticing that Missy has been very quiet, he snaps his fingers, thinking of the best way to get her active and happy again. *"And now, before you leave, I have put together some gifts for you and your family,"* says OMG proudly.

*"Did I hear gifts? presents for me?"* asks Missy immediately getting back to life, as OMG had so rightly, presumed. *"Where are the gifts? What am I getting? No need to gift-wrap. I need to go back to my Mumma and tell her of my adventures. And I need to pack for the King's coronation too."*

*"Patience, patience my dear child. Look at these* TRUNKS *I've got, for you to carry your presents in. There are an assortment of small* CUPCAKES, DESSERTS, *and* MOUSSE *for your friends.*

*The* CAKES *are for your teachers at school.*

*The* CUPCAKES *are for you.* ***They have purple filling,*** *as purple is one of your favourite colours.*

*SURPRISE SURPRISE! I have a* CELLPHONE *and* HEADPHONES *made from fresh raspberry mousse for you."*

*"Goodness gracious me! exclaims Missy. I cannot believe this."*

OMG carries on talking, *"the* PHONE *is for*

***your room. The*** HOT CHOCOLATE in ***a real chocolate*** CUP ***is for your journey back home.***

***Now, my birthday present for you – this gorgeous leafy*** PINATA. ***Breaking this open at your party may be sad. It has taken me five days to make all the candies***

***I have stuffed into it. You are sure to have the best birthday ever."***

Missy was beside herself with joy. She was so excited and happy. She neither knew what to say nor what to do.

Sensing this, OMG continued, ***"I have put in the shoes, bags, perfume and the dress for your Mumma.***

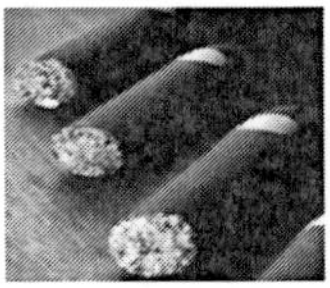

***I see there is a teeny-weeny bit of space. Would you like me to put these*** CIGARS ***in?"***

***"OH nono! Smoking is injurious to health and bad for the environment."***

***"Your gifts are packed and ready to go."***

***"Mister Master Magicmaker, as a thank you for everything, I have a poem especially for you.***

*"My chairs are chocolate muffins, my lamp shines chocolate light.*

*My piano is made of cocoa, if you're hungry, take a bite."*

*"Thank you, dear child. I am sad to see you go and will remember this day forever. I would like to tell you something very important.*

*Chocolate is rich, happy and active energy. It is easy to work with. Anyone can do that. But, to work with passion, love and pride in what you do, makes everything special, awesome, magical and wonderful. And for all the people of India I need to send this message"*

Suddenly, Missy feels someone shaking her furiously. It is Mumma saying, "Baby why are you so clumsily slumped in your chair? You will get a crick in your neck. Why are you not sleeping in your bed? Come, let me tuck you in with a hug and a kiss. Sweet dreams angel."

# Epilogue

SUNSHINE FOREVER AND ALWAYS is done. A happy ending……leading to a new beginning.

Izzy whizzy, now let's get busy, for it is time for a new adventure.

Yes, a new book is on the way. It will be in the *children's adventure novel* genre. One long story divided into several chapters, to make the read convenient.

I invite any and all of you to come write with me. Let us put our heads together and weave incredible stories. If you have any idea, any particular type of story you would like to read, we could make it happen.

Life, after all is a story. Let's make ours a bestseller!

Let us collect memories and moments, not things

Let us wander often and wonder always

Good Better Best, never let it rest. Till your good becomes better and your better becomes the BEST

Clever Class of 2024, we will meet again, soon. Meanwhile, should you need to write to me to co-author a book, to create poetry, to give ideas and story suggestions, to contribute to illustrations, please reach out to me on nina.nariman@gmail.com. Please do write BOOK as the subject.

Looking forward.